AWESOME
FACTS
FOR AMAZING
KIDS!

BY

ANTHONY RIPLEY

WORLD OF KNOWLEDGE
ANTHONY RIPLEY

Book Cover by Jason Stanhope

1st edition 2023

This book *is dedicated to Smart and Curious Kids everywhere!*

— Anthony Ripley

WELCOME to a hilarious journey through the amazing world of science, people and our incredible planet! Get ready to discover mind-blowing facts that will make you laugh, wonder, and maybe even a little bit smarter.

From the secrets of the universe to the quirks of the human body, this book is packed with fascinating information that will keep you entertained for hours. So grab a seat, buckle up, and let's get ready to embark on a wild ride through the world of fun and interesting facts!

Table of Contents

Table of Contents

Eight Crazy Laws that are Still Law

Don't Get Caught!

Are you ready to laugh out loud? In this article, we're going to explore 8 hilarious laws that are still on the books. Yes, you read that right, these are actual laws that still exist in some parts of the world. So, let's dive in!

1: No Singing in the Shower (New Hampshire, USA)

Yes, you read that right. According to the state law of New Hampshire, it's illegal to sing in the shower if you're naked. But don't worry, if you're wearing a bathing suit, you're in the clear. We're not sure who came up with this law or how they plan on enforcing it, but we do know that it's hilarious.

2: No Wearing High Heels Without a Permit (Carmel, California, USA)

If you're planning on strutting your stuff in high heels in the city of Carmel, California, you better make sure you have a permit. That's right, it's illegal to wear high heels without a permit. Apparently, this law was put in place to protect the city's sidewalks from damage caused by the sharp heels. But let's be real, who's going to take the time to get a permit just to wear high heels?

3: No Sleeping in a Fridge (France)

If you're ever in France and find yourself in need of a nap, make sure you don't crawl into a fridge to catch some Z's. It's illegal to sleep in a fridge in France. We're not sure why anyone would want to sleep in a fridge in the first place, but apparently, it was enough of a problem that the government had to make it illegal.

4: No Ketchup on Hot Dogs (Chicago, USA)

If you're a fan of ketchup on your hot dogs, you might want to avoid Chicago. According to a city ordinance, it's illegal to put ketchup on a hot dog if you're over the age of 18. Apparently, this is a serious offense in the Windy City. If you want to dress up your hot dog, you'll have to stick to mustard, relish, and onions.

5: No Fishing While Riding on the Back of a Giraffe (Florida, USA)

If you thought fishing was just a pastime for humans, think again. According to Florida law, it's illegal to fish while riding on the back of a giraffe. We're not sure why anyone would want to do this in the first place, but apparently, it was enough of a problem that the government had to make a law about it.

6: No Eating Fried Chicken With a Fork (Gainesville, Georgia, USA)

If you're a fan of fried chicken, you might want to avoid Gainesville, Georgia. According to a city ordinance, it's illegal to eat fried chicken with a fork. Apparently, the city wants to promote good old-fashioned finger-licking goodness. So, next time you're in Gainesville, make sure you leave your fork at home.

7: No Wearing a Suit of Armor to Parliament (UK)

If you're a knight in shining armr, you might want to think twice before heading to Parliament in the UK. According to an ancient law, it's illegal to wear a suit of armor to Parliament. We're not sure why this law was put in place, but we can only imagine the chaos that would ensue if everyone showed up in full armor.

8: No Walking Backwards While Eating a Donut (Oklahoma, USA)

If you're planning on enjoying a donut in Oklahoma, make sure you're walking forward. According to state law, it's illegal to walk backwards while eating a donut on a city street. We're not sure why!

The World's Tallest Person
Robert Wadlow Reached 8' 11"

Do you ever wonder how tall people can get? Well, in the case of Robert Wadlow, it seems the sky was the limit. Wadlow was the tallest man to have ever lived, and he was one of a kind.

Robert Wadlow was born in 1918 in Alton, Illinois, USA. He was a pretty normal-sized baby, but by the time he was six months old, he already weighed 30 pounds. That's more than double the weight of an average six-month-old baby! As he grew older, he didn't just get bigger, he got taller too. By the time he was eight, he was already over 6 feet tall. That's taller than most adults!

At age 13, Wadlow was already 7 feet 4 inches tall. That's almost as tall as a basketball hoop! As he grew taller, he also faced many challenges. Simple things like finding clothes and shoes that fit him became a real struggle. He also had to use a special walking stick to help him walk, as his legs were so long.

Despite the difficulties he faced, Wadlow was a very positive person. He loved meeting new people and traveling around the world. In fact, he even visited the White House and met President Franklin D. Roosevelt in 1936. He was also a popular attraction at fairs and exhibitions, where people would come from all over just to see him.

By the time he was 22 years old, Wadlow was officially declared the tallest man in the world. He stood at a staggering height of 8 feet 11 inches tall. That's almost as tall as a two-story building! Imagine having to look up that high just to talk to someone.

Sadly, Wadlow's life was cut short when he was just 22 years old. He developed an infection in his leg due to a brace he wore, and it quickly spread throughout his body. Despite receiving medical treatment, he passed away soon after. But even though he was only with us for a short time, he made a big impact on the world.

Wadlow's legacy still lives on today. He has been featured in books, movies, and even has a statue in his hometown of Alton, Illinois. His incredible height remains a world record to this day, and it's unlikely that anyone will ever reach his towering height again.

So, what made Robert Wadlow so tall? Well, it's all down to genetics. Wadlow inherited a rare condition called gigantism, which caused his body to produce too much growth hormone. This caused him to grow much taller than the average person.

Although being tall has its challenges, Wadlow made the most of his unique height and inspired people all over the world. He showed us that no matter what challenges we face, we can still live a full and happy life. So, let's raise our heads high, just like Robert Wadlow, and see what the world has in store for us.

The First Man on the Moon
Neil Armstrong Makes History

In 1969, something out of this world happened - literally! On July 20th, 1969, Neil Armstrong became the first man to set foot on the moon. And what an adventure it was!

Neil Armstrong was part of a team of three astronauts who were sent to the moon on the Apollo 11 mission. The other two astronauts were Buzz Aldrin and Michael Collins. These guys were the best of the best and had been training for this mission for years.

On the day of the mission, the whole world was watching. People were glued to their televisions, waiting for news about whether the mission would be successful or not. It was a tense moment for everyone, including the astronauts themselves.

As they got closer to the moon, Neil Armstrong and Buzz Aldrin got into a small lunar module that was going to take them down to the surface. The module was called the Eagle, which was a pretty cool name if you ask me.

But as they got closer and closer to the moon, they realized that things were not going according to plan. The surface of the moon was rougher than they had anticipated, and they were running out of fuel.

Neil Armstrong had to think fast. He took control of the module and guided it down to the surface himself. It was a bumpy ride, but they made it in the end.

As soon as they landed, Neil Armstrong uttered those famous words, "That's one small step for man, one giant leap for mankind." It was a historic moment that will be remembered forever.

But here's the thing - there's a conspiracy theory that says that the whole moon landing was faked. Can you believe that? People actually think that it was all just a big show put on by the government.

Now, I'm not saying that it was definitely real or definitely fake. But here are a few reasons why I think it was real:

First of all, there were thousands of people involved in the mission. Scientists, engineers, pilots, and more. Do you really think that all of those people would be willing to lie about something so big?

Secondly, there is physical evidence that the mission took place. There are rocks that were brought back from the moon that have been studied extensively. There are also photos and videos of the mission that have been analyzed in great detail.

Finally, there's the fact that we've been back to the moon several times since then. If the first moon landing had been fake, wouldn't someone have blown the whistle by now?

Anyway, back to the story. After Neil Armstrong and Buzz Aldrin had spent a few hours on the moon, it was time to head back to Earth. They took off in the Eagle and joined Michael Collins, who had been orbiting the moon in the Apollo 11 spacecraft.

The journey back to Earth was long and tiring. The astronauts were cramped in a small space, and they had to be careful with their supplies. But they made it back safely, and the whole world celebrated their success.

Neil Armstrong and Buzz Aldrin became instant celebrities. They traveled around the world, giving speeches and meeting with world leaders. They were hailed as heroes, and rightly so.

But here's the funny thing - Neil Armstrong was a pretty modest guy. He didn't like being in the spotlight, and he didn't think he was anything special. In fact, he once said that he was just "a lucky guy who happened to be in the right place at the right time."

Can you imagine that? The first man to walk on the moon, and he thought he was just lucky! I guess that just goes to show that even the most amazing people can be humble.

The Invention of the Automobile

Fast and Furious at 10 Miles and Hour

The invention of the automobile is a fascinating story, full of ups and downs, twists and turns, and maybe even a few speeding tickets. So buckle up, kiddies, and let's take a ride through history!

It all started back in 1769, when a Frenchman named Nicolas-Joseph Cugnot invented the first self-propelled vehicle. It was a steam-powered tractor that could move at a speed of about 2.5 miles per hour. Not exactly a sports car, but hey, it was a start!

Fast forward to 1885, and a German engineer named Karl Benz created the first practical automobile. It was powered by an internal combustion engine and could travel at a speed of about 10 miles per hour. People were so excited about this new invention that they started racing their cars against each other, just for fun. And so, the first car race was born!

But not everyone was thrilled about this new mode of transportation. In fact, some people thought it was downright dangerous. There were no stop signs, traffic lights, or even lanes on the road. It was chaos out there! So, in 1899, the first traffic law was passed in the United States. It required drivers to not exceed 12 miles per hour in the city and 15 miles per hour on country roads. Can you imagine going that slow?

As the automobile became more popular, more and more people wanted one. But they were expensive and not everyone could afford one. That's where Henry Ford comes in. In 1908, he introduced the Model T, which was the first car that was affordable for the average person. It cost $825, which was a lot of money back then, but still a lot less than other cars on the market.

But driving a car wasn't always easy. Before the invention of power steering, drivers had to use all their strength to turn the wheel. And before the invention of air conditioning, they had to roll down the windows to stay cool. Can you imagine driving a car in the middle of summer without air conditioning? Yikes!

Over the years, cars became faster, more powerful, and more luxurious. In the 1960s, muscle cars became all the rage. These were cars with big engines that could go really fast. People loved them so much that they even started naming them after animals. The Mustang, the Cougar, the Barracuda – you get the idea.

But as cars got faster, they also got more dangerous. In 1966, the U.S. government passed a law requiring all cars to have seat belts. And in 1970, the first airbags were introduced. These safety features have saved countless lives over the years.

Today, cars are more high-tech than ever before. Some can even drive themselves! But no matter how advanced they get, they all still have one thing in common: they need gas to run. And with climate change becoming a bigger and bigger problem, people are starting to look for alternatives. Electric cars are becoming more popular, and some car companies are even experimenting with cars that run on hydrogen.

So there you have it – the history of the automobile in a nutshell. It's been quite a ride, hasn't it? From steam-powered tractors to self-driving cars, we've come a long way in a relatively short amount of time. Who knows what the future holds? Maybe one day we'll be driving cars that fly! Or maybe we'll all be zooming around in jetpacks. One thing's for sure – it's going to be an exciting ride!

How America Became a Country

Or Why Americans Prefer Coffee to Tea

Once upon a time, a long, long time ago, America was just a bunch of colonies, which were like a bunch of grumpy siblings who didn't always get along. Each colony had its own rules, its own government, and its own way of doing things. But one day, they all decided to work together and become one big happy family. This is the story of how that happened.

In 1607, the first English settlement was established in Jamestown, Virginia. Other colonies soon followed, including Massachusetts, Connecticut, Rhode Island, New Hampshire, and Maryland. Each of these colonies was established by different groups of people, with different beliefs and values. Some were looking for religious freedom, while others were looking for a fresh start.

Over time, the colonies began to grow and prosper. They traded with each other, and with other countries, and they built schools, churches, and businesses. But they were still under the control of England, and England was getting pretty bossy.

In 1765, England passed the Stamp Act, which was a tax on all printed materials, including newspapers, books, and playing cards. The colonists were not happy about this, and they protested by boycotting British goods. This made England even angrier, and they responded with even more taxes and restrictions.

Things got really bad in 1773, when England passed the Tea Act. This allowed a British company to sell tea to the colonies without paying the usual taxes. The colonists were outraged, and in Boston, a group of men dressed up like Native Americans and dumped over 300 chests of tea into the harbor. This event, known as the Boston Tea Party, marked a turning point in the relationship between the colonies and England.

In 1775, the Revolutionary War began. The colonies formed an army, led by George Washington, and fought against England. It was a long and difficult war, but the colonies eventually emerged victorious.

On July 4, 1776, the Continental Congress adopted the Declaration of Independence, which declared that the colonies were no longer part of England. The document was signed by 56 brave men, who risked everything to create a new nation based on freedom, democracy, and equality.

But it wasn't easy. The new nation, called the United States of America, faced many challenges in its early years. There were conflicts with Native American tribes, wars with other countries, and economic struggles. But through it all, the American people persevered, and the country continued to grow and prosper.

In 1787, a group of delegates met in Philadelphia to create a new constitution, which would provide a framework for the government of the United States. The constitution established a system of checks and balances, which ensured that no one branch of government had too much power. It also included the Bill of Rights, which guaranteed certain freedoms to all Americans.

On March 4, 1789, the new government was officially inaugurated. George Washington was elected as the first president of the United States, and he served two terms, from 1789 to 1797.

Since then, America has continued to grow and evolve. It has faced many challenges, including wars, economic downturns, and social unrest. But through it all, the American people have remained resilient and determined, and the country has continued to be a beacon of hope and freedom to people all over the world.

The Loch Ness Monster
A Lot Going On Under the Surface

It is said, in the misty waters of Scotland's Loch Ness, there lived a creature so mysterious, so elusive, that many people believed it couldn't possibly be real. This creature, of course, was the Loch Ness Monster.

Now, some people say that the Loch Ness Monster is just a legend, like unicorns or dragons. But others swear they've seen the beast with their own eyes, and there have been countless photos, videos, and eyewitness accounts of Nessie over the years.

But let's be honest: the Loch Ness Monster is pretty funny. I mean, think about it - this giant sea monster that's supposedly been living in a lake for hundreds of years? It's like something out of a cheesy horror movie!

And yet, people are still obsessed with Nessie. There are entire books, TV shows, and websites devoted to trying to solve the mystery of the Loch Ness Monster. So, let's take a closer look at the real history of this mythical beast.

The first recorded sighting of the Loch Ness Monster dates all the way back to the 6th century, when a man named Saint Columba is said to have encountered a monster in the waters of the River Ness. According to legend, Columba ordered the creature to leave the area and it obeyed, disappearing beneath the waves and never to be seen again.

But it wasn't until the 20th century that the legend of the Loch Ness Monster really took off. In 1933, a man named George Spicer claimed to have seen a giant creature with a long neck and humps swimming across the lake. And from there, the sightings only grew more frequent.

In the years that followed, there were countless photos and videos of Nessie, many of which were later proven to be hoaxes. But that didn't stop people from believing in the Loch Ness Monster. In fact, some people became so obsessed with finding Nessie that they devoted their entire lives to the search.

One such person was Robert Rines, a scientist who spent years studying the Loch Ness Monster. In the 1970s, he even claimed to have captured images of Nessie on sonar, which he believed proved that the creature was real. But despite his best efforts, Rines was never able to find definitive proof of the Loch Ness Monster's existence.

Of course, that hasn't stopped people from having fun with the legend of Nessie. There are countless jokes and pranks about the Loch Ness Monster, from fake sightings to Nessie-themed souvenirs. And let's not forget the famous photo of Nessie's head and neck sticking out of the water, which has been parodied in everything from cartoons to t-shirts.

But despite all the fun and games, there's still a part of us that wants to believe in the Loch Ness Monster. Maybe it's the thrill of the unknown, or the hope that there's still something magical and mysterious left in the world.

So, is the Loch Ness Monster real? Well, that's a question that's likely to remain unanswered for years to come. But in the meantime, we can still have fun with the legend of Nessie, telling funny stories and enjoying the mystery of this mythical creature. And who knows? Maybe one day, we'll finally get to the bottom of this mystery and discover the truth about the Loch Ness Monster. Or maybe we'll just have to keep laughing and enjoying the ride.

The Invention of Motion Pictures

Hooray for Hollywood (and Paris)

Ages ao, people had to entertain themselves by doing things like playing outside, reading books, or just staring at the wall. It was a pretty boring time. But then, something amazing happened - the invention of movies!

Now, the invention of movies is a pretty funny story because, believe it or not, people used to think it was a silly idea. "Why would anyone want to watch moving pictures?" they said. "It's not like they're going to be better than real life!"

But some brave inventors didn't listen to the naysayers. They knew in their hearts that they could create something amazing, and they set out to do just that.

The first thing they had to do was figure out how to capture moving pictures. This was no easy task, mind you. They tried using all sorts of different techniques, like drawing pictures really quickly and then flipping through them, or using spinning disks to create the illusion of movement.

But finally, after years of trial and error, they discovered a technique that actually worked. They called it the "movie camera", and it was a pretty nifty piece of machinery if they do say so themselves.

With the movie camera in hand, the inventors could finally capture moving pictures, but there was one problem: they had no way to show them to anyone! They tried projecting the pictures onto walls, but it was too dark to see anything. They tried showing them on tiny screens, but the pictures were too small to make out.

Finally, they hit upon the idea of creating a "movie projector" - a machine that could take the pictures from the camera and blow them up onto a big screen. And lo and behold, the movies were born!

The very first movie ever made was called "Workers Leaving the Lumière Factory". It was a pretty boring movie, to be honest - just a bunch of workers leaving a factory, as the name suggests. But to people back then, it was a miracle. They had never seen anything like it before!

As word of the movies spread, more and more people started going to see them. They would sit in dark rooms for hours on end, watching pictures flicker on the screen. Some people found the experience mesmerizing, while others found it downright spooky. One thing was for sure, though - the movies were here to stay!

As the years went by, the movies got better and better. They started adding sound, which was a game-changer. People could now hear the characters talking, laughing, and singing. They also started adding color, which made everything look a lot more vibrant and exciting.

And of course, the movies gave us some of the greatest comedies of all time. Who can forget the antics of Charlie Chaplin, or the slapstick humor of the Three Stooges? These comedic geniuses made us laugh, cry, and everything in between.

But the movies weren't just about entertainment. They also played an important role in shaping the world we live in today. They helped to break down cultural barriers, allowing people from all over the world to share their stories and experiences with others. They also helped to educate people on important social issues, from civil rights to environmentalism.

Today, movies are still a huge part of our lives. We go to theaters, watch them on our phones, and binge-watch entire series on streaming services. And who knows what the future holds? Maybe one day we'll have movies that we can smell, taste, and touch!

So, as silly as it may seem to think about a world without movies, it's worth remembering just how much this invention has changed our lives. From classic comedies to epic dramas, from heartwarming romances to pulse-pounding action, movies have given us countless hours of entertainment - and they're a lot better than staring at brick walls!

William Shakespeare
Much Ado About Something

A long time ago, in England, there was a man named William Shakespeare. Now, William Shakespeare was a pretty interesting guy. He wrote a lot of plays and poems, and he's considered one of the greatest writers of all time. But there's a lot more to his story than just that!

First of all, let's talk about his name. "William Shakespeare" sounds like a pretty normal name, right? Well, back in his day, people spelled their names however they wanted. Some people think that "Shakespeare" might not even have been his real last name! Some historians think he might have gone by other names, like "Shakeshaft" or "Shakspere". We may never know for sure!

Now, William Shakespeare wrote a lot of plays - like, a lot. He wrote 37 of them, in fact! Some of his most famous plays include "Romeo and Juliet", "Hamlet", and "Macbeth". But did you know that he also wrote some pretty silly plays? That's right, he wasn't always a serious writer. He wrote comedies like "The Taming of the Shrew" and "A Midsummer Night's Dream", which were full of jokes, puns, and silly characters.

But here's the thing - a lot of people back then didn't really "get" his jokes. You see, Shakespeare wrote in a style called "Early Modern English", which is kind of like a different language than what we speak today. It had a lot of strange words and phrases that people back then would have understood, but that we might not understand now.

For example, in "Hamlet", one character says, "There's a divinity that shapes our ends, rough-hew them how we will." What does that even mean? Who knows! But people back then would have understood it perfectly.

But even if his jokes didn't always land, Shakespeare was still a pretty popular guy. He was a big deal in London, where he lived and worked. He hung out with some pretty fancy people, like Queen Elizabeth I and King James I. And he was really good at what he did - his plays were performed in theaters all over the city, and people loved them.

Now, there's a funny story about one of Shakespeare's plays. It's called "Macbeth", and it's a pretty spooky play about witches and murder and all sorts of scary stuff. Well, back when it was first performed, some people thought it was actually cursed! They believed that saying the name "Macbeth" in a theater would bring bad luck, so they called it "the Scottish play" instead.

And get this - there are even more superstitions surrounding Shakespeare's plays! For example, some people believe that saying "good luck" before a performance is actually bad luck, so they say "break a leg" instead. And some people think that it's bad luck to whistle backstage, because it sounds like you're calling a ghost. Isn't that crazy?

But here's the thing - even though Shakespeare wrote all those plays and poems, we don't actually know that much about his life. We don't even know exactly when he was born! Some people think he was born in 1564, while others think it might have been 1565 or even 1566. And we don't know that much about his family or his personal life, either. It's a bit of a mystery!

So there you have it - the history of William Shakespeare! He was a pretty interesting guy, with a lot of jokes and superstitions and mysteries surrounding him. But one thing's for sure - he was a really good writer, and his plays and poems are still taught in schools, and enjoyed by audiences the world over.

Thomas Edison Invents the Lightbulb

He Was Full of Bright Ideas

A long time ago, people used candles and oil lamps to light their homes. But one day, a man named Thomas Edison had an idea - what if we could make a lightbulb that would light up a room without all the mess and fuss of candles and oil lamps? And thus, the quest for the lightbulb began!

Now, Thomas Edison was a pretty interesting guy. He was an inventor, which means he liked to come up with new ideas and make things that no one had ever seen before. But here's the thing - he didn't always get it right on the first try. In fact, he failed a lot before he finally figured out how to make the lightbulb work!

At first, Edison tried using a material called platinum to make his lightbulbs. But platinum was really expensive, and it didn't work very well. So he kept experimenting with different materials until he finally found one that worked - a piece of carbonized bamboo.

But even after he found the right material, Edison still had a lot of work to do. He had to figure out how to make the carbonized bamboo last a long time, so that the lightbulb wouldn't burn out after just a few hours. And he had to figure out how to make the lightbulb safe, so that it wouldn't start a fire or shock anyone.

So, he tried all sorts of things. He tried putting the carbonized bamboo in a vacuum, to remove all the air and prevent it from burning out. He tried different filaments, to make the light last longer. And he tried different materials for the base of the lightbulb, to make it less likely to break or start a fire.

But here's the funny thing - Edison wasn't the only person trying to invent the lightbulb! There were actually a bunch of other inventors, all around the world, who were trying to make the same thing. And they were all racing to be the first one to invent it!

Now, Edison was a pretty competitive guy. He really wanted to be the first one to invent the lightbulb. So he did everything he could to make sure he was ahead of the game. He even had a team of assistants working for him, helping him test out different ideas and materials.

But here's the thing - Edison wasn't always the most honest guy. He actually had a lot of patents that he didn't really deserve. A patent is like a certificate that says you invented something, and no one else can make it without your permission. But sometimes, Edison would take credit for ideas that weren't really his, just so he could get the patent.

So, when Edison finally figured out how to make the lightbulb work, he was pretty excited. He knew that he was close to winning the race to invent it. But here's the funny thing - he actually didn't invent the lightbulb on his own! There were a bunch of other inventors who helped him along the way.

One of those inventors was a guy named Joseph Swan. He was actually working on the lightbulb at the same time as Edison, and he came up with a lot of the same ideas. But because he was working in England, he didn't get as much recognition as Edison did.

So, in the end, Edison did get credit for inventing the lightbulb. But it wasn't all him - he had a lot of help along the way. And even though he wasn't always the most honest guy, we still have to give him credit for coming up with a really important invention that changed the world!

Lewis and Clarke's Great Adventure

Across the American Wilderness

Lewis and Clarke were two famous explorers who set out to discover the great unknown wilderness of the west. Now, you might be thinking, "Why would anyone want to do that?" Well, Lewis and Clarke were on a mission - a mission to find a new trade route to the Pacific Ocean.

Their journey began in 1804, when they set out from St. Louis, Missouri, with a team of about 50 men. They were well-equipped, with guns, compasses, and maps, but they were also pretty clueless about what lay ahead of them.

Their first obstacle was the Missouri River. It was huge and wild, with rapids and currents that could easily flip their boats. But being the brave explorers that they were, Lewis and Clarke set out to conquer the river.

Now, Lewis and Clarke didn't exactly have the best luck with the river. They had some pretty close calls with rapids and sandbars, and one time they even got stuck in a mudbank for days. But they never gave up, and after many weeks of hard work, they finally made it to the other side of the Missouri.

But the Missouri River was just the beginning of their journey. They had to cross the Rocky Mountains, brave freezing temperatures, and fight off wild animals. And let me tell you, it wasn't easy.

One time, they came across a herd of buffalo. Now, you might think that buffalo are just big, dumb animals, but let me tell you, they are not to be messed with. These buffalo charged at Lewis and Clarke and their team, and they had to quickly climb a nearby tree to avoid getting trampled.

But being the resourceful explorers that they were, Lewis and Clarke came up with a plan to get the buffalo away from their camp. They set a fire and let the smoke drift towards the buffalo. The smoke made the buffalo think that there was danger nearby, and they ran away.

Lewis and Clarke also had to deal with the harsh winter weather. They were traveling through the mountains during the winter months, and it was cold. Really cold. But being the tough explorers that they were, they didn't let the cold slow them down.

They built makeshift shelters out of logs and animal hides, and they huddled together to keep warm. And they even invented a new kind of coat called a "capote," which was made out of animal hides and was great for keeping them warm in the cold weather.

But even with all their hardships, Lewis and Clarke never lost sight of their goal. They were determined to find a new trade route to the Pacific Ocean. And after many months of hard work, they finally made it.

On November 7th, 1805, Lewis and Clarke and their team finally reached the Pacific Ocean. They were the first Americans to cross the continent and reach the Pacific. And let me tell you, they were pretty excited about it.

They spent the winter on the coast, exploring the area and trading with the Native Americans. And they even built a fort, which they named Fort Clatsop.

But even with all their success, Lewis and Clarke still had to make the journey back to St. Louis. And let me tell you, it wasn't any easier the second time around.

They had to face the same obstacles they did on the way there - the Missouri River, the Rocky Mountains, the freezing temperatures. But they never lost hope, and after many more months of hard work, they finally made it back to St. Louis.

Lewis and Clarke's journey was a remarkable achievement. They explored unknown territory, discovered new animals and plants, and paved the way for future settlers to explore the west.

George Washington's Wooden Teeth

An Epically Bad Set of Chompers

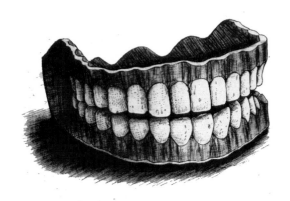

Once upon a time, in the land of the United States of America, there lived a man named George Washington. He was a great man who helped win the country's independence from the British. But there was one thing about him that many people didn't know about: his wooden teeth.

Yes, you read that right. George Washington had wooden teeth. Now, you might be thinking, "How did he eat with wooden teeth? Wouldn't they break?" Well, my dear reader, let me tell you the whole story.

First of all, let's clear up a misconception. George Washington didn't actually have wooden teeth. That's right, it's a myth! But why did people believe that he did? Well, let's go back in time to when George Washington was alive.

Back in the 1700s, people didn't have the best dental hygiene. They didn't brush their teeth twice a day like we do now, and they certainly didn't have fancy toothpaste or mouthwash. As a result, many people lost their teeth at a young age. George Washington was no exception.

By the time he was in his 20s, he had already lost several teeth. But don't worry, he didn't go around flashing a gummy smile. Instead, he had dentures made to replace his missing teeth.

Now, these dentures weren't like the ones you might see at your dentist's office today. They were made of all kinds of materials, like animal teeth, human teeth (ew!), and even ivory. But one thing they were definitely not made of was wood.

So how did the myth of George Washington's wooden teeth start? Well, some people say it was because the dentures he wore had a base made of wood. But that's not the same thing as having wooden teeth. Imagine if you had braces with metal wires, and someone called your teeth "metal teeth." That wouldn't be accurate, would it?

Another theory is that the myth started because George Washington had a fondness for a type of toothpaste that had a gritty texture. This toothpaste was made of things like crushed bones and oyster shells, and it could make your teeth look a little bit like they were made of wood. But again, that's not the same thing as actually having wooden teeth.

So, now that we've cleared up the myth, let's get back to the question at hand: how did George Washington eat with his dentures? Well, let's just say it wasn't easy.

First of all, the dentures didn't fit very well. They were bulky and uncomfortable, and they often rubbed against George Washington's gums, causing sores and infections. Can you imagine having to wear something like that all day long?

Secondly, the dentures didn't stay in place very well either. There were no fancy adhesives like we have today, so George Washington had to rely on gravity and his own muscles to keep them in place. This meant that he had to be very careful when he ate, lest the dentures fall out of his mouth!

And finally, the dentures didn't work very well either. Because they didn't fit properly, George Washington had trouble chewing his food. He often had to eat soft foods like porridge or soup, and he had to cut his meat into tiny pieces to make it easier to chew.

So, while George Washington didn't actually have wooden teeth, he did have to deal with some pretty uncomfortable and inconvenient dentures. But he didn't let that stop him from being a great leader and a hero of the American Revolution. In fact, he even had a set of dentures made specifically for his presidential inauguration in 1789!

The History of Spying
Who's Watching You?

Have you ever played a game of hide-and-seek? Well, that's kind of like what spying is all about. Spying is when one person tries to sneak around and gather information without being seen or caught. It's been around for thousands of years, and it's been used for all sorts of purposes – from stealing secrets to winning wars!

In ancient times, people would often use spies to gather information about their enemies. The first recorded instance of spying comes from ancient Egypt, where the pharaohs would send spies to gather information about their enemies. This was around 2000 BC! Can you imagine what it must have been like to spy back then? There were no fancy gadgets or cool spy gear – just good old-fashioned sneaking around.

Fast forward a few centuries to the 5th century BC, and we find ourselves in ancient Greece. The Greeks were experts at spying, and they even had a word for it: "scout." They would send scouts out to gather information about their enemies before going into battle. It was like having a secret weapon – they knew all the enemy's weaknesses before they even began fighting!

Jump ahead to 1066 AD, and we find ourselves in medieval times. Spying was still a popular tactic, but it was much harder than before. There were no phones or computers, so spies had to deliver their messages in person. This was really dangerous because they could be caught by the enemy at any time. Imagine having to sneak through enemy territory just to deliver a message!

Now let's fast forward to the 1500s, when Queen Elizabeth I ruled England. She was a big fan of spying and had a group of spies called the "Secret Service." They were responsible for gathering information about England's enemies and making sure that no one was plotting against the queen. One of the most famous spies from this time was Francis Walsingham. He was really good at his job and was known as the "spymaster" because he trained other spies and helped them to be successful.

The 1700s were a time of great change in the world of spying. This was when people began using secret codes to send messages. This made it much harder for enemies to intercept their messages. But, even with secret codes, spying was still a really dangerous job. Spies could be captured, tortured, and even killed if they were caught.

Now, we're up to the 1900s, and spying was getting even more high-tech. During World War I, both sides used airplanes to take pictures of enemy territory. These pictures were then used to plan attacks and gather information. It was like having a bird's-eye view of the enemy's position!

During World War II, spying became even more important. Both sides used spies to gather information about their enemies' plans. The most famous spy from this time was probably James Bond – he's a fictional character, but he's really cool!

These days, spying is still used by countries all over the world. The most famous spying organization is probably the CIA (Central Intelligence Agency) in the United States. They're responsible for gathering information about other countries and making sure that America is safe. They use all sorts of high-tech gadgets and cool spy gear to get the job done.

So, there you have it – a brief history of spying! It's been around for thousands of years and has been used for all sorts of purposes. Whether it's ancient Egypt or modern-day America, spies have always been an important part of gathering information and keeping countries safe. Just remember, if you're playing hide-and-seek with your friends, you might just be practicing to be a spy one day!

Special Effects in Movies

Monsters, Explosions, and Superheroes

Alright guys, get ready for a wild ride as we explore the history of special effects in movies! It all started back in the late 1800s when a guy named Georges Méliès accidentally discovered the magic of special effects.

In 1896, Méliès was filming a street scene when his camera jammed. When he started filming again, the scene had changed dramatically - people disappeared, others appeared out of nowhere, and it was all thanks to a clever use of stop-motion photography.

Méliès became obsessed with special effects and started experimenting with everything from double exposures to miniatures. In 1902, he made the first-ever science fiction film, "A Trip to the Moon," which featured aliens, rockets, and all sorts of crazy effects.

But it wasn't until 1925 when a movie called "The Lost World" was released that special effects really took off. This movie featured some of the first-ever stop-motion dinosaurs, which were created by a guy named Willis O'Brien.

From there, special effects continued to evolve and become more sophisticated. In the 1930s, movies like "King Kong" and "The Wizard of Oz" used groundbreaking techniques like matte paintings and rear projection to create realistic-looking worlds.

In 1939, a guy named Linwood Dunn invented the optical printer, which allowed filmmakers to combine different shots and add special effects like lightning or explosions.

The 1950s saw the rise of science fiction movies, which relied heavily on special effects to create aliens, spaceships, and futuristic worlds. Movies like "The Day the Earth Stood Still" and "Forbidden

Planet" used groundbreaking techniques like blue-screen and animatronics to create convincing otherworldly creatures.

By the 1960s, special effects had become a major part of the movie industry. "2001: A Space Odyssey" used models and special effects to create some of the most iconic space scenes in movie history, while "Planet of the Apes" used elaborate makeup and costumes to create believable ape characters.

The 1970s saw the rise of blockbuster movies, and special effects played a huge role in their success. Movies like "Star Wars" and "Close Encounters of the Third Kind" used groundbreaking techniques like motion control to create epic space battles and alien encounters.

In the 1980s and 1990s, special effects continued to evolve. "Terminator 2: Judgment Day" used groundbreaking CGI to create a liquid metal villain, while "Jurassic Park" brought dinosaurs to life with a mix of animatronics and CGI.

Today, special effects are a crucial part of almost every movie. From superhero movies to animated films, filmmakers use a variety of techniques to create convincing and realistic worlds.

Scott of the Antarctic
Britain's Greatest Explorer

In the early 1900s, everyone was talking about the South Pole. Some people said it was a frozen wasteland, while others believed there was a land of ice and snow waiting to be explored. One man who was determined to find out was Captain Robert Falcon Scott.

Scott was born in 1868 in England, and he was always fascinated by the idea of exploration. In

1901, he was chosen to lead an expedition to the South Pole. He and his team set off on their journey in 1902, but they quickly ran into trouble. The weather was terrible, and they had a hard time finding food.

Despite these challenges, Scott was determined to press on. He and his team made it to within 480 miles of the South Pole before they had to turn back. They were disappointed, but Scott knew that he would have to try again.

In 1910, Scott set out on his second expedition to the South Pole. This time, he was determined to be the first person to reach the Pole. He and his team faced even more challenges than before, but they kept going. They battled blizzards, crevasses, and extreme cold.

Finally, on January 17, 1912, Scott and four of his team members made it to the South Pole. They were ecstatic! They planted the British flag and took lots of pictures. However, their joy was short-lived. On their journey back to their base camp, they ran into more trouble.

Food and fuel were running low, and the weather was getting worse. To make matters worse, one of the team members, Edgar Evans, fell ill and was slowing them down. Despite Scott's best efforts to help him, Evans died on February 17.

Scott and his remaining team members continued on, but things continued to go wrong. The weather was unrelenting, and the men were getting weaker and weaker. Eventually, Scott and his two remaining team members, Lawrence Oates and Edward Wilson, became trapped in their tent during a blizzard.

They knew they were going to die, so they wrote letters to their loved ones and waited for the end. Scott's last diary entry was on March 29, 1912. His final words were, "We shall stick it out to the end, but we are getting weaker, of course, and the end cannot be far."

Scott and his team members died in their tent, but their legacy lived on. They were hailed as heroes for their bravery and determination. Even today, people remember their incredible journey to the South Pole.

Scott and his team faced a lot of challenges that they could have avoided if they had planned better. It's also important to remember that nature is powerful, and we need to respect it. Finally, we can learn that even if we don't achieve our goal, we can still be proud of what we accomplished. Scott and his team didn't make it to the South Pole first, but they still made history with their incredible journey.

How to Build a Radio
Make Your Own Radio Receiver

Building your own radio may seem like a tricky task, but with a few everyday objects and some basic knowledge, you can create your very own radio! Here's what you'll need:

Materials:

- A toilet paper roll
- A few feet of insulated wire
- A pencil or pen
- A razor blade or scissors
- A small piece of aluminum foil
- An earphone or small speaker

Step 1: Build the Tuning Coil

To start, take the toilet paper roll and wrap the insulated wire around it tightly from one end to the other. Leave a few inches of wire free at each end. This is called the tuning coil, and it will be used to pick up radio signals.

Step 2: Build the Capacitor

Next, take the pencil or pen and wrap the wire tightly around it to make a coil. Slide the coil off the pencil or pen and wrap a piece of aluminum foil around it. This is your capacitor, which will help tune your radio to specific frequencies.

Step 3: Connect the Coil and Capacitor

Take the ends of the insulated wire from the tuning coil and connect them to the capacitor. Twist the wire ends together to make a solid connection.

Step 4: Build the Detector

Take the razor blade or scissors and scrape off the insulation from one end of the wire. This will be your detector, which will convert the radio signals into sound.

Step 5: Connect the Earphone or Speaker

Take the earphone or small speaker and connect it to the other end of the wire from the detector. Twist the wire ends together to make a solid connection.

Step 6: Tune In

Now that your radio is built, it's time to tune in to some stations! Move the capacitor around the coil to find different frequencies. You may need to adjust the razor blade or scissors to find the best signal. Once you've found a good station, adjust the volume by moving the earphone or speaker closer or farther away from the detector wire.

And that's it! With just a few everyday objects, you've built your very own radio. Who knows what kind of music, news, or sports you'll be able to pick up with it!

The History of Skateboarding
Skate Hard or Go Home

Skateboarding has become one of the coolest and most popular sports in the world. But did you know that skateboarding actually started out as a way for surfers to practice their moves when the waves were flat? Let's take a look at the history of skateboarding and how it evolved into the exciting sport we know and love today.

The earliest known skateboard was made in the 1940s by some California surfers who wanted to continue their surfing fun on land. They attached roller skate wheels to a board and started experimenting with different ways to ride it. The first skateboards were very basic and didn't have the cool designs and features of modern-day skateboards.

In the 1950s, skateboarding really took off as a sport. Skateboarders began performing tricks and jumps on ramps, and the first skateboard competitions were held. The first professional skateboarders also emerged during this time.

However, by the 1960s, skateboarding had hit a bit of a slump. Many cities had banned skateboarding due to safety concerns, and it was no longer seen as a legitimate sport. But then in the 1970s, a group of skateboarders in Southern California began experimenting with new tricks and styles that would change the face of skateboarding forever.

These skaters, who became known as the Z-Boys, would ride their boards on empty swimming pools, creating a whole new style of skateboarding that was all about speed, agility, and creativity. The Z-Boys became famous for their innovative tricks, and their style of skateboarding became known as "vertical" skating.

In the late 1970s and early 1980s, skateboarding continued to grow in popularity, and new companies started to produce more sophisticated and advanced skateboards. Skateparks also began to spring up all over the world, providing skaters with a safe and controlled environment to ride in.

In 1984, skateboarding was finally recognized as a legitimate sport when it was included in the Summer Olympics. This helped to bring skateboarding even more into the mainstream, and many new skateboarders were inspired to take up the sport.

Today, skateboarding is enjoyed by millions of people all over the world. Professional skateboarders like Tony Hawk and Nyjah Huston have become household names, and skateboarding competitions like the X Games are watched by millions of people every year.

If you're interested in getting into skateboarding, there are a few things you'll need to know. First, you'll need to get a skateboard. There are many different types of skateboards available, so it's important to find one that's right for you. You'll also need some safety gear, such as a helmet, knee pads, and elbow pads.

Once you have your skateboard and safety gear, it's time to start practicing. Start by learning the basics, such as how to balance on the board and how to push off. Once you've got those down, you can start experimenting with different tricks and moves.

One important thing to remember when skateboarding is to always be safe. Skateboarding can be dangerous, so it's important to wear your safety gear at all times and to practice in a safe environment.

Skateboarding has come a long way since those first California surfers attached wheels to a board. It's now a thriving sport enjoyed by people of all ages and skill levels. Whether you're a seasoned pro or a beginner just starting out, skateboarding is a fun and exciting sport that's sure to provide you with hours of thrills and excitement. So grab your board and hit the pavement – it's time to start shredding!

How Birds Fly
They Don't Just Wing It

Birds have always fascinated humans with their ability to fly. They can soar high up in the sky, swoop down to catch prey, and even perform acrobatic stunts. But how do they do it? Let's take a closer look at the science behind bird flight.

The first thing to know is that birds have very light bodies, which makes it easier for them to take off and stay in the air. Their bones are hollow, and filled with air sacs that help them stay buoyant. In fact, some bird bones are so thin and fragile that they could easily break if they weren't filled with air!

Another important factor in bird flight is their wings. Birds have wings that are specially adapted for flight, with strong muscles and flexible joints that allow them to move their wings up and down, back and forth, and even twist them in different directions. When a bird flaps its wings, it creates lift, which helps it stay in the air.

But how do birds know when and where to flap their wings? This is where their incredible senses come into play. Birds have excellent eyesight, which helps them navigate through the air and spot prey. They also have a special sense called "proprioception," which allows them to sense the position and movement of their wings and body.

Of course, flying isn't just about flapping your wings and hoping for the best. Birds have to be able to control their flight, to make sure they don't crash into anything or get blown off course by the wind. To do this, they use a combination of body movements and wing adjustments, constantly making small corrections to their flight path.

One of the most impressive things about bird flight is their ability to soar without flapping their wings. Many birds, like eagles and hawks, can catch thermals, which are updrafts of warm air that rise from the ground. By circling within these thermals, birds can gain altitude without using any energy, allowing them to travel long distances with minimal effort.

So, now that we know a bit more about how birds fly, is it possible for humans to do the same? While we don't have wings like birds, we can use technology to help us fly. Airplanes, helicopters, and even hot air balloons all use principles of aerodynamics to stay in the air.

But for those who want to experience the thrill of flying without a machine, there is one option: skydiving. By jumping out of a plane and freefalling through the air, skydivers can experience the sensation of flight, even if it's only for a short time.

So, the next time you see a bird soaring through the sky, remember all the amazing adaptations that allow them to fly. And who knows, maybe someday humans will find a way to take to the skies just like our feathered friends!

What Are Boogers Even For?

And Why Can't They Taste Better?

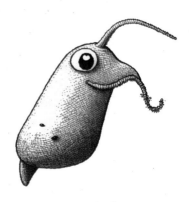

Boogers. We all have them, and we've all wondered why they exist. Are they just dried-up snot? A protective layer for our noses? A secret weapon for flinging at our enemies? Let's take a closer look at these mysterious little blobs and find out what they're really for.

First, let's talk about what boogers actually are. You know that sticky, slimy stuff that comes out of your nose when you have a cold? That's mucus, and it's made up of water, protein, and a bunch of other stuff that helps keep your nose moist and trap dirt and germs before they can get into your body. Gross, right? But it's important stuff.

Now, when the mucus in your nose dries out, it turns into a booger. But why does it dry out in the first place? Well, one reason is that the air we breathe is usually pretty dry, especially in the winter when we're all cranking up the heat. That dry air can suck the moisture out of our noses, leaving us with crusty, booger-filled nostrils.

But wait, there's more! Boogers actually serve a purpose beyond just annoying us and making us feel gross. They're like tiny little filters, catching all sorts of dirt and germs that try to enter our bodies through our noses. Think of them as the bouncers at the door of your body, keeping out the riffraff.

Of course, like any good filter, boogers eventually need to be replaced. That's why we're always picking our noses (don't pretend like you don't do it too). When you pick your nose, you're removing the old, dirty boogers and making room for fresh, clean ones to take their place.

But don't get too excited about your booger-removing habit. Picking your nose too much can actually cause irritation and bleeding, which can make it easier for germs to get into your body. Plus, let's be real, it's just kind of gross.

So, there you have it, folks. Boogers may be slimy and gross, but they're actually doing an important job of keeping us healthy.

The Story of the FBI
"Fidelity, Bravery, Integrity"

The FBI, or Federal Bureau of Investigation, is a U.S. government agency that is responsible for investigating and preventing crime across the country. The FBI has been around for over 100 years, and has had a fascinating history full of interesting stories.

In 1908, Attorney General Charles Bonaparte founded a small group of special agents within the Department of Justice to investigate federal crimes. The group was initially known as the Bureau of Investigation, and consisted of just 34 agents. They were tasked with investigating violations of federal law, such as fraud, bank robbery, and land fraud.

Over the years, the Bureau of Investigation grew in size and scope, and in 1935 it was renamed the Federal Bureau of Investigation. It was also given the authority to investigate a wide range of crimes, including espionage and sabotage.

One of the most famous cases the FBI ever worked on was the investigation into the kidnapping of Charles Lindbergh's baby in 1932. The baby was taken from his crib in the middle of the night, and the kidnapper left a note demanding a ransom of $50,000. The FBI was called in to investigate, and they quickly identified a suspect named Bruno Hauptmann. Hauptmann was eventually convicted of the crime and executed.

During World War II, the FBI worked closely with other government agencies to investigate and prevent espionage and sabotage. They also played a key role in investigating war crimes committed by the Nazis.

In the 1950s, the FBI turned its attention to organized crime, and began a campaign to dismantle the Mafia. The FBI's efforts resulted in the imprisonment of many high-ranking mobsters, and helped to weaken the Mafia's grip on the country.

The FBI has also been involved in investigating civil rights violations. In the 1960s, the FBI worked closely with civil rights activists to investigate hate crimes and other forms of discrimination. They played a key role in bringing about social change and promoting equal rights for all Americans.

In more recent years, the FBI has been involved in investigating cyber crimes, including identity theft and computer hacking. They also played a key role in investigating the terrorist attacks of September 11, 2001, and have since been involved in preventing further acts of terrorism.

Throughout its history, the FBI has faced criticism and controversy. Some people have accused the agency of overstepping its bounds and violating people's civil rights. Others have questioned the FBI's tactics and the methods they use to investigate crimes.

Despite the criticism, the FBI remains an important and vital part of the U.S. government. Its agents work tirelessly to investigate crimes and protect the American people, and they have helped to bring many dangerous criminals to justice over the years. Whether you love them or hate them, there's no denying that the FBI has had an interesting and important role in American history.

The Curse of Tutankhamun

Mummy Dearest

The curse of Tutankhamun is one of the most intriguing mysteries of ancient Egypt. It's a story about an Egyptian pharaoh who died at a young age, and the curse that supposedly plagued those who entered his tomb. Are you ready to learn about this spooky tale? Great, let's go!

Tutankhamun, also known as King Tut, became pharaoh of Egypt when he was only nine years old. He ruled for about ten years before his death at age 19. When he died, he was buried in a grand tomb in the Valley of the Kings in Egypt.

But in 1922, a group of archaeologists led by a man named Howard Carter found King Tut's tomb. They had been searching for years, and when they finally uncovered it, they found a treasure trove of artifacts and treasures.

However, as soon as they entered the tomb, strange things began to happen. Some of the workers got sick, and others reported seeing strange visions. The newspapers of the time ran wild with stories about the "curse of the pharaohs" and how it had been unleashed upon those who dared to disturb Tutankhamen's resting place.

Despite the rumors and fear, the archaeologists continued their work, and the treasures they found inside the tomb were nothing short of amazing. There were gold masks, jewelry, and even furniture. It was one of the most significant archaeological discoveries of the time.

But as the months went by, it seemed that the curse was indeed taking its toll. Lord Carnarvon, one of the wealthy benefactors who helped fund the excavation, died suddenly, and his death was attributed to the curse. Newspapers ran headlines such as "Pharaoh's curse strikes again!" and "Tut's vengeance claims another victim!"

The newspapers had a field day with the story, and people all over the world were fascinated by the idea of a curse from ancient Egypt haunting the archaeologists.

But did the curse really exist? Well, there is no scientific evidence to support the idea that a curse was responsible for the deaths or illnesses of those who entered Tutankhamen's tomb. In fact, most of the people associated with the excavation went on to live long and healthy lives.

So what really happened? Well, it's possible that the deaths and illnesses were just coincidences. After all, the tomb was sealed for thousands of years, and there were likely all sorts of bacteria and viruses lurking inside.

Another possibility is that some of the deaths were caused by the toxic fumes that were released when the tomb was first opened. There were lots of chemicals and substances in the tomb, and it's possible that some of them were dangerous when exposed to air.

Whatever the case may be, the curse of Tutankhamun remains a fascinating story to this day. People love to be scared, and the idea of a mummy's curse is just too intriguing to ignore. Whether or not the curse was real, it's a fascinating piece of history that continues to capture our imaginations.

The World's Most Dangerous Snakes

Snakes. Why Did it Have to be Snakes?

If you're ever wandering through the wilderness, it's best to know which snakes to avoid. Some snakes may look cool, but they can also be deadly. Here's a funny guide to the world's most dangerous snakes that you definitely don't want to mess with.

1. Black Mamba

The black mamba may sound like a cool name for a snake, but it's actually one of the deadliest snakes in the world. They're found in Africa and can grow up to 14 feet long. Not only are they venomous, but they can also strike multiple times in just one attack. You definitely don't want to run into one of these while on a safari.

2. Inland Taipan

This snake, also known as the "fierce snake," is found in Australia and has the most toxic venom of any snake in the world. However, they're also pretty shy and would rather avoid humans than attack them. But still, it's probably best to give them their space.

3. King Cobra

The king cobra is found in Asia and is the world's longest venomous snake, measuring up to 18 feet long. They're also known for their aggressive behavior and can rear up to a third of their body length when threatened. Don't mess with the king cobra unless you want to end up on the menu.

4. Eastern Brown Snake

This snake is found in Australia and has venom that can cause paralysis and cardiac arrest. It's also responsible for the most snakebite deaths in Australia. So, if you ever find yourself down under, watch your step.

5. Fer-de-Lance

The fer-de-lance is found in Central and South America and is known for its deadly venom that can cause tissue damage and internal bleeding. It's also one of the most aggressive snakes in the world, so don't try to pet this one.

6. Tiger Snake

This snake is found in Australia and is responsible for the second most snakebite deaths in Australia. Its venom can cause paralysis and respiratory failure. And as you may have guessed from its name, it's also pretty aggressive.

7. Russell's Viper

The Russell's viper is found in Asia and is responsible for the most snakebite deaths in India. Its venom can cause internal bleeding, kidney failure, and even death. So, if you're ever in India, watch out for this slithery killer.

8. Puff Adder

The puff adder is found in Africa and is responsible for the most snakebite deaths on the continent. Its venom can cause tissue damage, bleeding, and even death. And, as if that wasn't enough, it also has the fastest strike of any snake in the world. So, if you see one of these, run the other way!

9. Black-Backed Jackal

Wait, what? A jackal isn't a snake! Well, that's true, but this jackal is known to eat venomous snakes like the black mamba, king cobra, and puff adder without being affected by their deadly venom. So, if you ever see a black-backed jackal, maybe follow it around and see if it leads you to any cool snakes.

10. Your Mom

Just kidding! Your mom is not a dangerous snake. But seriously, always be careful when encountering snakes in the wild. Remember to give them their space, and if you do get bitten, seek medical attention immediately.

So, there you have it, kids! Stay safe out there, and maybe invest in a pair of snake-proof boots.

Albert Einstein

20th Century Brainiac

Albert Einstein was born on March 14, 1879, in Ulm, Germany. As a child, Einstein was fascinated by the mysteries of the universe, and he spent many hours daydreaming and imagining what it would be like to travel through space.

Einstein's parents were concerned about his lack of interest in school, and they worried that he might not succeed in life. However, Einstein was determined to follow his own path, and he began to study physics and mathematics on his own.

In 1905, when Einstein was 26 years old, he published a series of papers that would change the course of science forever. One of these papers introduced the theory of special relativity, which explained how time and space are intertwined and how they affect the behavior of light.

Einstein's theory of special relativity challenged the established beliefs of the scientific community, and it was met with skepticism and criticism. However, over time, the theory was proven correct through experiments and observations.

In 1915, Einstein published another groundbreaking paper, this time introducing the theory of general relativity. This theory expanded on the ideas of special relativity, and it explained how gravity works and how it affects the fabric of space and time.

Einstein's theories were not only revolutionary, but they were also difficult to understand for many people. However, Einstein was determined to share his ideas with the world, and he spent much of his life writing and speaking about his theories.

Einstein became a cultural icon, and he was known not only for his genius, but also for his wild hair and his love of the violin. He was a pacifist, and he was known for his strong beliefs in social justice and equality.

In 1921, Einstein received the Nobel Prize in Physics for his work on the photoelectric effect, which explained how electrons are ejected from atoms when they are exposed to light.

Throughout his life, Einstein continued to push the boundaries of science and to inspire new generations of scientists. His legacy lives on today, and his theories continue to shape our understanding of the universe.

Albert Einstein passed away on April 18, 1955, at the age of 76. However, his ideas and his legacy will continue to inspire and shape the world for generations to come.

The Spooky History of Halloween

Trick or Treat?

Halloween is one of the most popular holidays in the world, celebrated annually on October 31st. But where did this spooky holiday come from? Let's take a trip down history lane and find out!

The origins of Halloween can be traced back to an ancient Celtic festival called Samhain, which was celebrated on November 1st. The Celts believed that on this day, the boundary between the living and the dead became blurred, allowing ghosts to roam freely among the living.

To ward off these spirits, the Celts would light bonfires and dress up in scary costumes, hoping to scare away the ghosts. They would also leave offerings of food and drink for the spirits, hoping to appease them and avoid any mischief.

When the Romans conquered the Celts, they blended their own festival of the dead, called Feralia, with Samhain. This helped to spread the celebration of Samhain throughout the Roman Empire.

Fast forward to the Middle Ages, and Halloween had become a Christian holiday known as All Hallows' Eve. It was the night before All Saints' Day, a day to honor all the saints and martyrs of the Christian church.

But Halloween as we know it today really took off in America in the 19th century, when Irish immigrants brought their traditions to the new world. They introduced the idea of carving pumpkins, which they had done in Ireland with turnips, to make jack-o'-lanterns.

The name Halloween is actually a contraction of "All Hallows' Eve." It was first used in the 16th century, but didn't become popular until the 20th century.

Trick-or-treating, a popular Halloween activity among kids, actually has its roots in a medieval tradition called "souling." On All Souls' Day, poor people would go door-to-door asking for food in exchange for prayers for the dead.

In America, trick-or-treating became popular in the 1920s and 1930s, as a way for communities to come together and celebrate the holiday. Kids would dress up in costumes and go door-to-door asking for candy, shouting the famous phrase "trick or treat!"

Of course, Halloween isn't all fun and games. There are plenty of spooky tales and legends associated with the holiday, such as the legend of the Headless Horseman or the story of Dracula.

One of the most famous Halloween stories is the legend of the Salem Witch Trials. In 1692, a group of young girls in Salem, Massachusetts, claimed to be possessed by witches. The hysteria spread, leading to the arrest and execution of 20 people accused of witchcraft.

But Halloween is also a time for fun and creativity. Kids love to dress up in costumes, and there's no shortage of spooky decorations and treats to enjoy.

If you're looking to have some Halloween fun, why not try carving your own pumpkin? You can find pumpkin carving kits at your local store, or you can try using a template and a sharp knife.

If you're feeling adventurous, you can even try making your own Halloween treats, such as spooky cupcakes or witch's brew punch.

And of course, Halloween wouldn't be complete without some spooky stories. Gather your friends around and take turns telling scary tales by candlelight, or watch a classic horror movie together.

So whether you're trick-or-treating, carving pumpkins, or just enjoying some spooky fun, Halloween is a holiday that has something for everyone. And now that you know a little more about its history, you can appreciate the holiday even more. Happy Halloween!

Baseball Cards
A History of Collecting

Baseball cards have been a popular collectible for over a century, but their history is more interesting than you might think. The first baseball cards were made in the 1860s, but they weren't quite like the ones you see today. Back then, they were actually advertisements for things like cigarettes and soda. Yup, you read that right - people used to get baseball cards with their smokes and soda pops.

But it wasn't until the late 1800s that baseball cards really started to take off. That's when a company called Allen & Ginter began producing cards that featured popular baseball players. These cards were still used as advertisements, but they quickly became more popular as collectibles.

In the early days of baseball cards, they were printed on thick cardboard and featured colorful lithographic images of the players. They were often packaged with other products, like tobacco or candy, and were sometimes given away for free.

One of the most famous baseball cards ever made is the T206 Honus Wagner card. This card was made in 1909 and is extremely rare - only about 50 are known to exist. The reason it's so rare is because Honus Wagner himself didn't want his image to be used on the cards. Legend has it that he didn't want kids to buy cigarettes just to get his card, so he asked the company to stop making them.

Another famous baseball card is the 1952 Topps Mickey Mantle card. This card is considered by many to be the holy grail of baseball cards, and a mint condition one can sell for hundreds of thousands of dollars.

As baseball became more and more popular, so did baseball cards. By the 1930s and 1940s, companies like Goudey, Play Ball, and Bowman were producing cards with color photos of the players. And by the 1950s, Topps had become the dominant company in the baseball card industry.

One of the interesting things about baseball cards is that they often reflect the technology and trends of their time. For example, in the 1960s, Topps started printing cards with a peel-off backing, so kids could stick them in albums. And in the 1970s, cards featured holograms and 3-D effects.

But as with any collectible, the value of baseball cards is based on supply and demand. Some cards are extremely rare and valuable, while others are worth only a few cents. The most valuable cards are usually those from the early days of baseball cards, before they became mass-produced.

Baseball cards have also become an important part of popular culture. They've been featured in movies and TV shows, and have even been the subject of songs. There's even a famous episode of the TV show "The Simpsons" where Bart gets a valuable baseball card and accidentally trades it away for a pack of gum.

Today, there are still companies making baseball cards, but the industry has changed a lot. There are more types of cards now, including ones with pieces of game-worn jerseys or autographs. And instead of just featuring baseball players, cards can also feature other sports, like basketball or football.

Baseball cards are still a beloved collectible for many people. Whether you're a serious collector or just enjoy looking at the pictures, there's something special about holding a piece of baseball history in your hands.

The First Airplane
A Long Time Getting Off the Ground

In the early 20th century, the idea of flying was nothing more than a pipe dream. That is, until two brothers from Ohio, named Orville and Wilbur Wright, came along and changed the course of history.

It all started in 1899, when the Wright brothers began tinkering with bicycles in their spare time. They were fascinated by the idea of creating a machine that could fly, and they were determined to make it happen.

In 1901, the Wright brothers began experimenting with gliders. They would take their gliders to a nearby hill and jump off, hoping to catch some air. But more often than not, they would come crashing back down to Earth.

Despite their failures, the Wright brothers refused to give up. In 1903, they designed and built their first airplane, which they called the Wright Flyer.

On December 17, 1903, the Wright brothers finally achieved their dream of flight. They took off in their airplane and flew for a distance of 120 feet, staying in the air for a total of 12 seconds. It was a small flight, but it was a giant leap for mankind.

The Wright brothers continued to improve upon their design, and by 1905, they had built an airplane that could stay in the air for up to 38 minutes.

Their achievements did not come without some hilarity, though. In fact, the Wright brothers had some pretty funny mishaps along the way.

For example, in 1904, the Wright brothers decided to take their airplane to Europe to show it off. However, they quickly discovered that their airplane was too big to fit through the doors of the train they were traveling on.

Not to be deterred, the Wright brothers dismantled their airplane and reassembled it on the train platform. But when they tried to take off, they crashed into a fence and damaged their plane.

Another time, Orville Wright took a reporter for a ride in his airplane. As they were flying, the reporter's hat flew off and landed in the propeller, causing the plane to crash. Luckily, no one was injured, but it was definitely a close call.

Despite their mishaps, the Wright brothers' accomplishments inspired a generation of inventors and aviators. They paved the way for commercial air travel and changed the world forever.

In fact, their legacy still lives on today. The Wright Brothers National Memorial in North Carolina is a testament to their achievements, and people from all over the world visit it to pay homage to the famous brothers.

So, the next time you hop on a plane to go on vacation, remember the Wright brothers and their journey to flight. Who knows, maybe your flight will be as funny as one of theirs!

Where Did Hamsters Come From?

Cute and Cuddly Desert Critters

Hamsters are small, cute and fluffy animals that have become popular pets around the world. But how much do you know about their history? Let's dive into the world of hamsters and learn about their origins!

Hamsters were first discovered in 1839 by a zoologist named George Robert Waterhouse. He was exploring Syria and found a small, furry creature that he named Cricetus auratus, or the golden hamster. These hamsters were found living in burrows in the desert and were able to survive in harsh conditions by storing food in their large cheek pouches.

It wasn't until 1930 that hamsters were domesticated and became popular as pets. A professor named Israel Aharoni caught some golden hamsters and brought them back to Israel. He successfully bred them in captivity and soon, they became a popular pet all around the world.

The first pet hamsters were quite expensive, and only wealthy people could afford them. But by the 1950s, they had become more affordable and were sold in pet stores all over the world.

Hamsters come in many different breeds and colors, but the most common is the golden hamster. Other breeds include the dwarf hamster, the Russian hamster, and the Chinese hamster. Each breed has its own unique characteristics, such as the dwarf hamster being smaller and more social than the golden hamster.

Hamsters are popular pets because they are easy to take care of and are quite active. They are also nocturnal, which means they are most active at night. This makes them a great pet for kids who are in school during the day.

If you're thinking about getting a hamster as a pet, there are a few things you need to know. First, hamsters need a lot of space to run around and play. A cage with plenty of toys and hiding places is essential. Second, hamsters need a balanced diet that includes fresh vegetables, fruit, and seeds. Finally, hamsters need to be handled gently and often so they can become used to human interaction.

Hamsters have become popular pets all around the world, but they are also used in scientific research. Because hamsters are small and easy to handle, they are often used in experiments to test drugs and medical treatments.

In addition to being great pets and scientific subjects, hamsters have also played a role in popular culture. In the 1990s, the animated series Hamtaro became a hit with kids. The show followed the adventures of a group of hamsters and their owner, Laura.

Hamsters have also inspired many internet memes and viral videos. One popular video features a hamster eating a tiny burrito, while another shows a hamster running on a wheel that's been modified to look like a giant Mario Kart.

In conclusion, hamsters have come a long way since their discovery in the Syrian desert in 1839. From being wild animals to becoming beloved pets and even scientific subjects, hamsters have made an impact on the world. So the next time you see a cute, fluffy hamster, remember their fascinating history!

Why Does Soda Have Bubbles?

Is it to Tickle Our Noses?

Have you ever wondered why your favorite soda is all fizzy and bubbly? Well, buckle up because we're about to take a wild ride into the history of fizzy drinks!

It all started in the late 1700s when a man named Joseph Priestley was experimenting with different gases. One day, he discovered a gas that made water taste really weird. It turned out to be carbon dioxide, a gas that is all around us but is usually odorless and colorless. Priestley thought it might be a good idea to mix this gas with water to create a bubbly drink. And thus, the first fizzy drink was born!

However, it wasn't until the early 1800s that people started to really take notice of this fizzy drink. A man named Jacob Schweppe, who was a Swiss watchmaker, created a machine that could produce carbonated water in large quantities. He started selling his sparkling water to the public and it became a huge hit!

But why does carbon dioxide make drinks fizzy? Well, it's all about pressure. When you open a can of soda, you're releasing the pressure that has built up inside the can. This causes the carbon dioxide gas to escape from the liquid and form bubbles. The more pressure there is, the more bubbles there will be. That's why if you shake up a can of soda, it will explode with fizz!

So why do people like fizzy drinks so much? It's all about the sensation! When you drink a fizzy drink, the bubbles tickle your tongue and make your mouth feel all tingly. Some people even say that the bubbles make the drink taste better! Plus, fizzy drinks are usually sweeter than still drinks, which makes them even more appealing to some people.

But did you know that not all fizzy drinks are created equal? Some drinks are naturally fizzy, like sparkling water or champagne. These drinks get their bubbles from a natural fermentation process, where yeast eats sugar and produces carbon dioxide as a byproduct. Other drinks, like soda or beer, have carbon dioxide added artificially to create the bubbles.

So what's the difference between naturally fizzy drinks and artificially carbonated drinks? Well, naturally fizzy drinks are usually healthier because they don't have any added sugar or artificial flavors. Artificially carbonated drinks, on the other hand, can be loaded with sugar and other unhealthy additives. So while fizzy drinks might be fun to drink, it's important to remember to drink them in moderation!

Now, you might be wondering how you can make your own fizzy drinks at home. Well, there are a few ways you can do it! One way is to buy a home carbonation machine, which allows you to add carbon dioxide to your own drinks. Another way is to make your own naturally fizzy drinks, like kombucha or ginger beer. These drinks require a bit more effort to make, but they're usually healthier and more delicious than artificially carbonated drinks.

So there you have it, the wild and wacky history of fizzy drinks! Who knew that a simple gas could create such a sensation in our mouths? Next time you pop open a can of soda or sip on some sparkling water, remember the science behind the fizz!

Area 51

The TOP SECRET Government Base

Have you ever heard of Area 51? It's a secret government base located in the middle of the Nevada desert. And when we say secret, we mean really secret. So secret, in fact, that the government didn't even acknowledge its existence until 2013. But what exactly goes on at Area 51? Let's find out!

Area 51 was established in 1955 as a testing site for experimental aircraft. This was during the Cold War, when the United States and the Soviet Union were in a race to build the most advanced planes. The government needed a remote location to test their top-secret planes, and the middle of the desert seemed like the perfect spot. But as you might imagine, testing experimental aircraft isn't the most exciting thing in the world. So, how did Area 51 become so famous?

Well, over the years, rumors started to spread about the kind of things that were going on at the base. Some people claimed that the government was hiding evidence of extraterrestrial life. Others said that they were testing advanced weapons that could destroy entire cities. And then there were those who believed that Area 51 was home to a secret underground bunker, where the government was preparing for the end of the world.

Of course, the government denies all of these claims. According to them, Area 51 is simply a testing site for experimental aircraft. But if that's the case, why is it so heavily guarded? Why are there signs warning that deadly force is authorized if you cross the boundary? And why have there been so many reports of strange lights and sounds coming from the area?

These are all questions that people have been asking for years. And while we may never know the true purpose of Area 51, that hasn't stopped people from speculating. In fact, the base has become so famous that it's inspired countless movies, TV shows, and even video games.

But what do we really know about Area 51? Well, for starters, we know that it's located on a remote part of the Nevada desert, about 80 miles north of Las Vegas. The base is surrounded by miles of empty desert, which makes it the perfect location for testing top-secret aircraft. The base itself is made up of a series of hangers, runways, and other buildings, all designed to keep the experimental planes hidden from prying eyes.

One of the most famous stories about Area 51 involves a supposed UFO crash in Roswell, New Mexico, in 1947. According to some conspiracy theorists, the government recovered an alien spacecraft from the crash and took it to Area 51 for study. But again, the government denies all of these claims, saying that there is no evidence to support the idea of extraterrestrial life.

Despite the government's denials, Area 51 continues to fascinate people around the world. In fact, every year, thousands of tourists flock to the area to try and catch a glimpse of the secret base. But be warned, if you try to get too close, you might be met with a team of heavily armed guards who aren't afraid to use force to protect the base.

So, what's the truth about Area 51? Well, that's a question that might never be answered. But whether you believe that the government is hiding evidence of extraterrestrial life or simply testing experimental planes, one thing is for sure – Area 51 will always be one of the world's most fascinating mysteries.

We hope you enjoyed reading about this mysterious base and all the crazy rumors that surround it. Just remember, if you ever find yourself in the middle of the Nevada desert, keep an eye out for flying saucers and little green men!

The History of Baseball
America's National Pastime

Are you ready to step up to the plate and learn about the history of America's favorite pastime? Baseball has been around for over a century and has brought joy, tears, and plenty of funny moments to fans all over the world. So grab some peanuts and Cracker Jacks and let's get started!

Baseball's origins can be traced back to the 18th century in England, where a game called "rounders" was played. However, it wasn't until the mid-19th century that baseball as we know it began to take shape in the United States. The first recorded baseball game took place in Hoboken, New Jersey on June 19, 1846. The game was played by the Knickerbocker Base Ball Club and ended with a score of 23-1. Ouch, that's a rough loss!

In the early days of baseball, the game was played much differently than it is now. For example, instead of a pitcher throwing overhand, the ball was delivered underhand, and there were no balls or strikes. Batters were allowed to ask for high or low pitches, and if the pitcher couldn't deliver, the batter got a walk. Can you imagine if that rule still existed today? Pitchers would be walking batters left and right!

Another interesting fact about the early days of baseball is that fielders didn't wear gloves. That's right, they caught the ball with their bare hands! It wasn't until the 1870s that gloves began to be used. In fact, the first baseball glove was invented by Charles Waite, who was a pitcher for the St. Louis Brown Stockings. His glove was made of leather and looked more like a workman's glove than a modern baseball glove.

As baseball grew in popularity, so did the number of teams and leagues. The National League was founded in 1876 and was followed by the American

League in 1901. The two leagues would eventually merge to form Major League Baseball (MLB), which is the organization that oversees professional baseball in the United States and Canada today.

One of the most famous moments in baseball history took place on April 8, 1974, when Hank Aaron hit his 715th home run. This broke the record held by Babe Ruth and solidified Aaron's place in baseball history. But did you know that Aaron received death threats and hate mail while he was chasing the record? Some people didn't want to see a black man break Babe Ruth's record, but Aaron persevered and became a legend.

Of course, baseball isn't just about the players and their records. There are also plenty of quirky traditions and superstitions that have developed over the years. For example, some players believe that it's bad luck to step on the foul line when entering or exiting the field. Others have lucky socks or hats that they wear during games.

Another strange tradition is the "rally cap." This is when fans or players turn their baseball cap inside out or wear it backward in the hopes of inspiring their team to come back from a losing position. Does it actually work? Who knows, but it's a fun way to show your support!

Finally, we can't talk about the history of baseball without mentioning one of the sport's most famous curses: the Curse of the Bambino. This curse supposedly began in 1920, when the Boston Red Sox traded Babe Ruth to the New York Yankees. The Red Sox wouldn't win another World Series until 2004, leading many fans to believe that they were cursed for giving up the Great Bambino. Thankfully, the curse was finally broken, and Red Sox fans could finally breathe a sigh of relief.

So there you have it, the history of baseball in a nutshell. It's a game that has captured the hearts and imaginations of people for over a century, and it shows no signs of slowing down. Whether you're a die-hard fan or a casual observer, there's no denying the impact that baseball has had on American culture and beyond.

Why Birthday Cakes?

Because They're Delicious!

Ah, the delicious and iconic birthday cake! Who doesn't love blowing out candles and eating a slice of cake on their special day? But have you ever wondered how the tradition of birthday cake started? Let's dive into the history of birthday cakes!

Back in ancient Greece, people would celebrate the birthdays of their gods and goddesses with a cake made of honey and wheat. The cake was round and symbolized the moon, and candles were placed on it to represent the glow of the moon.

Fast forward to the 18th century, and the tradition of birthday cakes began to take shape in Germany. Germans would celebrate the birthdays of their children with sweetened bread dough, molded into the shape of a baby. These cakes were called Geburtstagorten, which translates to "birthday cakes."

However, birthday cakes as we know them today didn't become popular until the 19th century in Western cultures. Bakers began to experiment with cake recipes and added new ingredients like butter and sugar, which made cakes lighter and fluffier. This made it easier to add layers of frosting and decorations to the cake.

By the early 20th century, birthday cakes were a staple in many households, and cake decorating became an art form. People would go all out with elaborate designs, and even put candles on the cake, just like in ancient Greece.

But why do we blow out candles on birthday cakes? This tradition has its roots in ancient Greece as well. The Greeks believed that smoke from the candles would carry their prayers and wishes to the gods. Today, we blow out candles and make a wish for good luck in the coming year.

The world's largest birthday cake ever made was created in 1989 in Fort Payne, Alabama. The cake weighed a whopping 128,238 pounds and measured 128 feet long. It took over two weeks to bake and used 16,209 pounds of sugar and 470 gallons of frosting.

Nowadays, there are many different types of birthday cakes, from chocolate to vanilla to ice cream cakes. Some people even get creative with their cakes and make them into different shapes or designs, like a favorite animal or cartoon character.

In some cultures, birthday cakes are not the norm. For example, in China, people traditionally eat a long noodle dish called "yi mein" on their birthday to symbolize a long life. In Mexico, a sweet bread called "pan dulce" is often served instead of cake.

No matter what type of cake or tradition you prefer, one thing is for sure: birthday cakes have been bringing joy and celebration for centuries. So next time you blow out your candles, remember the ancient Greeks who started it all with their honey and wheat cake.

Isaac Newton and Gravity
A Hit Upside the Head

Isaac Newton and gravity: the story of how one apple changed everything

Isaac Newton was one of the greatest scientists who ever lived. He was born in 1643 in England, and he spent most of his life thinking about why things fall down.

You might be thinking, "What's so interesting about things falling down?" But trust me, Isaac Newton knew there was more to it than that.

One day, when Isaac was sitting under an apple tree, an apple fell on his head. Now, most people would have just said, "Ouch!" and moved on with their day, but not Isaac Newton. No, he started thinking about why the apple fell down instead of up.

After a lot of thinking and experimenting, Isaac Newton figured out something amazing. He discovered that there was a force that made things fall down, and he called this force "gravity."

Now, you might be thinking, "Well, duh! Everyone knows about gravity!" But back in Isaac Newton's day, no one had ever thought about gravity before. Isaac was the first person to realize that there was a force that pulled things down to the ground.

Isaac Newton was so excited about his discovery that he wrote a book about it called "Philosophiæ Naturalis Principia Mathematica." Now, that might sound like a really boring book, but trust me, it's not. It's full of all kinds of cool math and science stuff, like calculus and the laws of motion.

In his book, Isaac Newton explained how gravity worked. He said that every object in the universe was attracted to every other object by a force called gravity. The bigger the object, the stronger the force of gravity. That's why the Earth has a strong force of gravity – it's a big object!

Isaac Newton's discovery of gravity was a big deal. It helped scientists understand how the universe works, and it led to all kinds of new discoveries and inventions. For example, without Isaac Newton's understanding of gravity, we wouldn't have things like airplanes or spaceships.

But here's the funny thing about Isaac Newton and gravity. Even though he was one of the greatest scientists who ever lived, he wasn't always the most graceful person. In fact, there's a story that he once accidentally poked himself in the eye with a needle while he was experimenting with optics.

So, just because you're not the most coordinated person in the world, it doesn't mean you can't be a great scientist like Isaac Newton. After all, he discovered one of the most important things in the universe, and he did it by getting hit in the head with an apple!

How Big is the Universe?

Pretty, Pretty Big...

Have you ever looked up at the night sky and wondered how big the universe really is? Well, get ready to have your mind blown, because the universe is way bigger than you can possibly imagine!

Let's start with the basics: the universe is everything around us, including all the planets, stars, and galaxies. And when we say "big," we mean really big. In fact, the universe is so big that we measure it in something called "light-years."

Now, a light-year is the distance that light travels in one year, and light travels at an incredible speed of about 186,000 miles per second! That's really fast.

To put it in perspective, if you could travel at the speed of light, you could go around the entire Earth 7.5 times in just one second.

So, if the universe is so big that we have to measure it in light-years, how big is it exactly? Well, scientists estimate that the observable universe, which is everything we can see with our telescopes, is about 93 billion light-years across. That's a lot of zeros!

But wait, it gets even crazier. The observable universe is just a tiny fraction of the entire universe. In fact, scientists believe that the universe is infinitely large and may even be expanding at an accelerating rate.

Now, you might be wondering, if the universe is so big, how did it all begin? Well, that's a great question. Scientists believe that the universe began with a huge explosion called the Big Bang, about 13.8 billion years ago. This explosion created everything in the universe, including all the stars and galaxies.

Speaking of stars and galaxies, did you know that there are billions of them in the universe? That's right, billions! And each one is unique and beautiful in its own way. Some stars are huge, like the red supergiant Betelgeuse, which is so big that it would stretch beyond the orbit of Jupiter if it were in our solar system. Others are tiny, like the white dwarf star Sirius B, which is only about the size of the Earth.

And galaxies are just as fascinating. They come in all shapes and sizes, from spirals to ellipticals to irregulars. Our own Milky Way galaxy is a spiral galaxy, and it's home to hundreds of billions of stars, including our own Sun.

But wait, there's more! The universe is also filled with mysterious things like black holes, dark matter, and dark energy. Black holes are areas in space where the gravitational pull is so strong that nothing, not even light, can escape. Dark matter is an invisible substance that makes up most of the mass in the universe, even though we can't see it. And dark energy is a force that's causing the universe to expand at an accelerating rate.

So, there you have it, folks. The universe is incredibly big, and it's filled with all sorts of amazing things that we're still learning about. Who knows what other mysteries and wonders are waiting to be discovered out there in the vastness of space?

And the next time you're feeling small and insignificant, just remember: you're part of this amazing, infinite universe, and that's pretty darn cool.

The First Video Games

Time to Level Up

Once upon a time, in the not-so-distant past of the early 1970s, people were just beginning to discover the magical world of video games. Before that, folks were too busy playing hopscotch and jacks to care about this newfangled "computer" stuff.

But then, along came a man named Ralph Baer. He was an inventor, and he loved to tinker with things. One day, while sitting in his workshop, he had a brilliant idea. "What if," he thought, "I could create a game that you could play on your TV?"

And so, he got to work. He created a box that could be plugged into a TV, and he called it the "Brown Box." It wasn't the prettiest thing in the world, but it was the first-ever video game console.

The Brown Box had a few simple games on it, like ping pong and a shooting game. People were amazed. They had never seen anything like it before. They flocked to Ralph Baer's workshop to see the Brown Box in action.

Soon, other people started getting interested in video games, too. A company called Atari saw the potential and created a game called Pong, which was a huge hit. It was basically just like ping pong on the Brown Box, but people loved it.

After that, the floodgates opened. More and more companies started making video games. There was Space Invaders, Pac-Man, Donkey Kong, and so many others. Each game was more creative and exciting than the last.

Kids loved video games because they were so much fun. They could play them for hours and never get bored. Parents loved them because they kept their kids occupied and out of trouble. And the video game industry grew and grew, until it became a multi-billion dollar business.

Nowadays, video games are everywhere. You can play them on your phone, your computer, and even on your watch. But it all started with one man's brilliant idea, a Brown Box, and a dream.

So next time you're playing your favorite video game, think about Ralph Baer and all the hard work that went into creating it. And remember, it all started with a simple idea and a whole lot of determination.

How Do Spiders Walk on Walls?

It's All in the Legwork

Spiders are amazing creatures that can be found all over the world. These creepy crawlies can be pretty scary, but did you know that they have a superpower? That's right, they can walk on walls and ceilings like it's no big deal! How do they do it? Let's find out.

To understand how spiders can walk on walls, we first need to know a little bit about how they stick to surfaces. Spiders have tiny hairs on their legs called setae, and at the end of each seta is a small, triangular structure called a spatula. These spatulae allow spiders to cling to surfaces using a force called van der Waals force. This force is basically an attraction between molecules, and it's what makes your hand stick to a wall when you press it against it.

So, with their tiny spatulae and van der Waals force, spiders can easily climb up walls and hang out on ceilings. But how do they stay attached when they're upside down? Well, spiders have an extra trick up their sleeves (or rather, up their legs). They can actually change the way they use their setae depending on the surface they're climbing on.

On a flat surface like a wall, spiders use all of their setae to create as much surface area as possible. This maximizes the van der Waals force and allows them to stick to the wall. But when they're hanging upside down, they only use the tips of their setae to create a smaller surface area. This helps to reduce the van der Waals force and allows them to stick without falling off.

But spiders don't just use their setae to stick to surfaces. They also use their muscles to grip onto the surface. When a spider climbs, it actually uses a combination of sticking and gripping to move along. This helps to give them more control and stability when they're walking on walls and ceilings.

Now, you might be wondering why spiders don't just fall off of walls all the time. After all, van der Waals force is pretty weak compared to other forces like gravity. The answer is that spiders are actually really good at sensing when they're starting to slip. If they feel like they're losing their grip, they can quickly adjust their legs to stick more firmly to the surface.

So there you have it, folks! Spiders can walk on walls and ceilings because they have tiny spatulae on their legs that allow them to use van der Waals force to cling to surfaces. They also use their muscles to grip onto the surface, and they're really good at sensing when they're starting to slip. Pretty cool, right? Just don't look too closely the next time you see a spider crawling on your wall!

The Legend of the Boogeyman

Ask Him Yourself. He's in Your Closet

Once upon a time, long before TikTok and Snapchat, kids used to be scared of the boogeyman. They believed that this mythical creature lived in their closets, under their beds, or in the dark corners of their bedrooms. But where did this spooky legend come from?

The legend of the boogeyman dates back to medieval times when people would tell stories about a monster called the "bogey." This creature was said to be a goblin-like monster that would come out at night and kidnap children who misbehaved.

Over time, the name "bogey" evolved into "boogeyman," and the legend spread across Europe and eventually made its way to America.

The boogeyman was said to be a shape-shifter, capable of taking on any form to scare children. Some stories describe him as a tall, thin man with long, spindly fingers and a deep, menacing voice. Others say he is a furry creature with glowing eyes and sharp claws.

Despite his scary appearance, the boogeyman was said to be easily defeated. All children had to do was face their fears and stand up to him. This would make him disappear forever.

Today, the boogeyman is more of a silly story that parents tell their children to get them to behave. But, the legend lives on, and the boogeyman continues to scare kids all around the world.

In some cultures, the boogeyman has a different name. In Spain, he is known as "El Cuco," in Italy as "Il Babau," and in Russia as "Babayka." But no matter where you go, the boogeyman remains a universal legend that has been passed down for generations.

So, the next time you feel scared at night, remember that the boogeyman is just a legend. All you have to do is face your fears, and he will disappear just like that!

Who's Smarter? Cats or Dogs?
SPOILER ALERT: Probably Dogs

Are dogs smarter than cats? It's a question that has puzzled humans for centuries. Some people say dogs are smarter because they can learn tricks and do things like fetch and play dead. Others say cats are smarter because they're independent thinkers and don't need as much attention. So, who's right? Let's take a closer look.

First, we have to define what "smart" means. Is it the ability to learn new things? The ability to solve problems? The ability to communicate with humans? Or is it something else entirely?

When it comes to learning new things, dogs definitely have the advantage. They're eager to please their owners and will do just about anything for a treat. That's why they're used as service animals and police dogs. Cats, on the other hand, are notoriously stubborn and independent. They're less likely to respond to training, and when they do, it's usually on their own terms.

But what about problem-solving? This is where cats shine. They're natural hunters and have to use their wits to catch prey. They're also great at figuring out how to get into places they shouldn't be. Dogs, on the other hand, tend to rely on their owners to solve problems for them.

Communication is another important aspect of intelligence. Dogs are known for their ability to understand human language and respond to commands. Cats, on the other hand, communicate more through body language and vocalizations. They're not as good at understanding human language, but they're great at letting you know when they want something.

So, who's smarter? It's hard to say. Dogs and cats are intelligent in different ways. Dogs are great at learning new things and communicating with humans, while cats are great at problem-solving and communicating with other cats.

But let's be real, when it comes down to it, who's the smartest animal? Humans, of course! We can do things like read and write, invent new technologies, and build skyscrapers. Plus, we can train both dogs and cats to do pretty much anything we want them to do. So, maybe the real question is, are dogs and cats smarter than humans? That's a debate for another day.

In conclusion, dogs and cats are both intelligent animals in their own way. Whether you're a dog person or a cat person, there's no denying that these furry friends bring joy and companionship to our lives. So, instead of arguing about who's smarter, let's just appreciate them for who they are.

Why Kids are Awesome!
The Undeniable Truth

Let's face it, kids are awesome. Sure, they may throw tantrums, spill juice on the carpet, and refuse to eat their vegetables, but they also have a unique ability to bring joy and excitement to the world around them. From their infectious laughter to their boundless imagination, kids are truly amazing creatures. But what is it that makes kids so awesome? Let's explore the undeniable truth.

First and foremost, kids are full of wonder and curiosity. They see the world with fresh eyes and an unbridled sense of exploration. They ask questions that adults have long forgotten to ask and find joy in the simplest things, like jumping in puddles or blowing bubbles. This sense of wonder keeps kids open to new experiences and fuels their thirst for knowledge.

In addition, kids have an incredible capacity for resilience. They fall down, get back up, and keep going with an enthusiasm that can put adults to shame. They don't dwell on failure or setbacks, but rather see them as opportunities to learn and grow. This resilience allows kids to face challenges with a sense of determination and optimism.

Another reason why kids are awesome is their ability to make friends easily. They don't see social hierarchies or differences in background, but rather connect with others based on common interests and a shared sense of fun. This natural ability to build relationships and create community is a gift that should not be underestimated.

Of course, one of the biggest reasons why kids are awesome is their boundless creativity. Kids have a knack for thinking outside of the box and coming up with ideas that are imaginative, whimsical, and sometimes downright hilarious. They can turn a cardboard box into a spaceship or a stick into a magic wand. Their creativity is a reminder to adults to approach life with a sense of playfulness and joy.

Finally, kids have an infectious energy and enthusiasm that can light up a room. Their excitement is contagious and can inspire others to see the world with fresh eyes. Kids remind us to not take life too seriously and to find joy in the everyday moments.

So, there you have it. The undeniable truth about why kids are awesome. Whether it's their sense of wonder, resilience, social skills, creativity, or energy, kids have a unique ability to make the world a better place.

Thanks for reading this book filled with interesting and funny facts about science, people, and the world around us! We hope you had a blast reading it and learned something new.

If you enjoyed the book, we would greatly appreciate it if you could take a moment to leave a review on Amazon. Your review will help other kids discover this book and join in the fun! Thank you again for joining us on this wild and wacky journey of discovery!

— Anthony Ripley

WORLD OF KNOWLEDGE
ANTHONY RIPLEY

Made in United States
North Haven, CT
25 April 2023

35856758R00076